I0480506

About Author

Sanjay Grover is an industry leader, Certified & Seasoned Project Manager and Coach. He is having diversified leadership experience in Indian and Global Pioneer Organizations like IBM and Tata group.

He did his Masters in Computer Applications. He has more than 30 years of experience of Leading large, complex, global & local projects in Telecom, Real Estate, Education, Aviation, Manufacturing industry domains.

Author's Note

Hello, Welcome to my new course "Project Management Practices". I have designed and developed this course specifically for aspirant Project Managers and Project Managers based on my learning & experience in delivering various projects in India, Europe and US in last more than 30 years while working with Indian and Global companies.

Project Delivery is the core function of any project. We deliver our projects effectively and contribute to the success of the project stakeholders, clients, and to our organization.

Change is inevitable.   Change is the fact of the life and project. Projects by their nature change regularly. I have given a great emphasis on handling the changes.

This course introduces you to some of the most valuable "Practices" I learnt and following in all my projects. I am sure these practices will also help you to deliver your project with excellence. These practices have been created to adopt in multiple scenarios, including Agile, Traditional and Hybrid projects.

I have tried to cover the concepts of executing Agile and traditional projects and then taken a simple example to elaborate all the practices as a part of this course.

By using these best practices, you can be assured to bring the maximum impact – on quality, schedule, and on project financial.

Wish you a great and happy learning!

I am sincerely thankful to my son, Prateek, who contributed to the success of the physical creation of the book, he was instrumental in editing, graphic designing and creation of book cover.

Sanjay Grover

Index

Chapter 1 - Learning objectives

After completing this course, you will be able to -

Understand, Learn and Apply Project Management practices for the project success while managing your project.

Create a Project Management System Summary (PMSS). You can use this summary for project related communications with stakeholders.

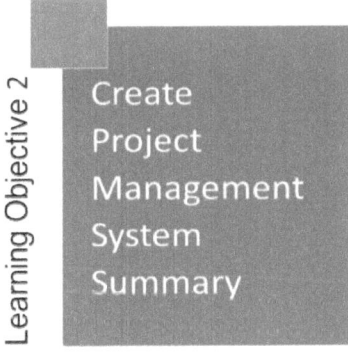

Chapter 2 - Benefits of using Standard Project Management Methodology

There are the 3 key benefits of using Standard Project Management Methodology.

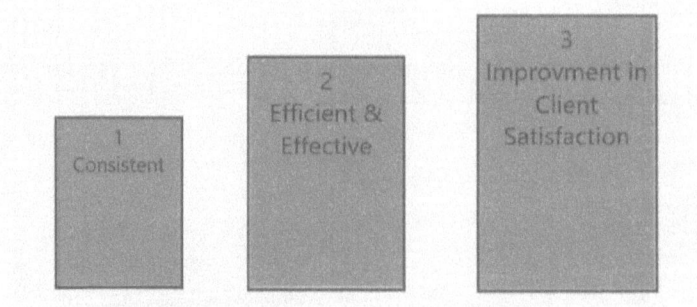

1. Consistent

Consistently executing projects allows you to improve each time. Deploying consistent approaches to iterations and schedules, issues, risks, impediments and blockers, and financial management, increase the opportunities for successful delivery. Using standard project management method will help you repeat your successes in project delivery.

Organizations can compare their projects across the portfolios and identify trends to improve delivery across all their projects.

Clients know what to expect from the organization when it delivers projects.

The same methods and procedures that resulted in successfully delivering one project, can be repeated in other projects.

2.   Efficient and effective

Standard Project management Method provides a roadmap which you can easily follow from project start to close.

Business organizations can apply lessons learned from previous projects to subsequent Projects for continued improvements and effectiveness.

Flexibility in applying project delivery practice improvements to new project and in-flight projects increases. As business changes, Standard project management method is a solid foundation for execution which can be used on any project, at any time.

3.   Improvement in Client Satisfaction

By using standard Project Management method, you will have a better chance of completing your projects on time and within the budget which almost always results in satisfied clients and stakeholders. Communication of status, issues, risks, impediments, blockers and financials keep the client involved and aware of any required adjustments to iterations, schedule, costs, or scope.

Pervasive, common issues with delivery can be analyzed and resolved at the organization level and then can be enabled in future projects may be in stages.

Standard Project management method is one of the guarantees for project success. Delivering projects successfully helps the organization in getting the more opportunities in the marketplace. Good performance leads to more opportunities to succeed. Consistent success in delivering projects using Project Management Method means clients, Organization and you will be benefited.

Chapter 3 - Managing Agile and Traditional projects

You can use standard Project Management Method to manage all types of projects, both agile and traditional ones.

In agile projects, you start with high-level requirements, and as you start delivering on an iterative basis, new learning emerges, and you get greater clarity on requirements.

Agile has three key points to note:

- The first is that you should expect the requirements to evolve over time as you learn more about them through delivery.

- The second is not to expect to put requirements under formal change control.

- The third is not to commit to deliver on a predetermined scope.

In an agile project, fixed time might be a constraint for the project manager if the contract type is of shared commitments and it is important to recognize its impact on delivery of urgent business needs. The project manager must get a clear view of how many iterations are needed to deliver against a Minimum Viable Product (MVP), and once committed, must manage fixed resources to deliver at the determined cost.

In a traditional project, the requirements are fully specified at the beginning and stay fixed throughout the project lifecycle.

Time and resources are variable: the project manager can decide to review the time initially projected for tasks and change the assigned resources to the project to reduce cycle time.

1. Main concepts for an agile project

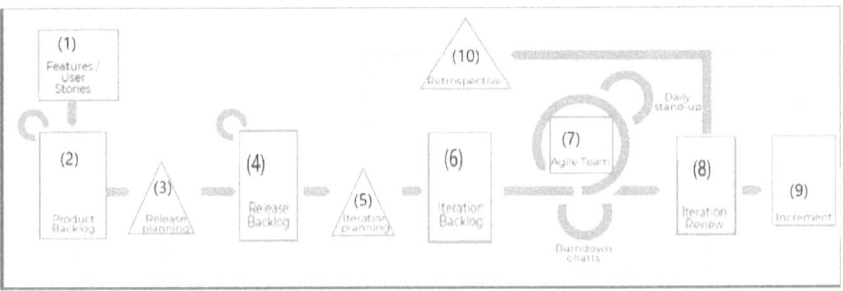

Features / User Stories (1)

In the agreement with the client, Customer asks the service provider to build a product.

For the product, you get features of varying sizes from multiple stakeholders.

Traditional requirements are termed as features, which are further decomposed into user stories in agile and are defined from the user's point of view.

Product Backlog (2)

The product backlog is the single source of requirements to build for the product.

It evolves over time and is dynamic. It constantly changes to identify what the product needs to be appropriate, competitive, and useful. The Product Owner is responsible for the product backlog, including its content, availability, and ordering.

Release Planning (3)

Once you have the product backlog, the team needs to plan which user stories will be in a particular release of our product.

Release backlog (4)

The release backlog is a subset of the product backlog. It consists of the selected features or user stories from the release planning that are planned to be delivered in the coming release, typically on a three- to six-month horizon.

Iteration Planning (5)

Iterations, also called sprints, are short timeboxed periods that a cross-functional team works in to complete a work scope of highest possible value to a ready-to-ship state. The iteration length on projects is usually 2 weeks, depending on the ability to collect feedback and incorporate it. Iterations on different projects might range from 1 – 4 weeks.

The specific product backlog items for the team to work on in the next iteration are agreed at the iteration planning, which occurs at the beginning of each iteration. During iteration planning, the team conducts the next level of just-in-time detailed planning.

Iteration Backlog (6)

The collection of user stories that are executed within the iteration.

The goal of each iteration is to get a subset of the release backlog to a ship-ready state. So, at the end of each iteration, you should have a fully tested product with all the features of the iteration.

Agile Team (7)

[1] The agile team is led by the Iteration Manager (or Scrum Master). The Iteration Manager is a servant leader. The Iteration manager is not only managing the project, but instead facilitates the events and removes any impediments that the team faces so that they can complete their iteration goals.

The Iteration Manager sets up meetings, monitors the work being done, and facilitates release planning. The Project Manager might take this role, but larger projects usually have a different Iteration Manager.

The rest of the team has similar roles as for other development processes, including for developers and testers.

Daily Stand-up (7.1)

The daily stand-up meeting is a fast-paced stand-up meeting where team members quickly list the work they have completed as well as emerging issues since the last meeting.Meeting daily ensures the work is always on track and any major issues are dealt with as soon as they are known. The meeting duration should not exceed 15 minutes.

[1] What is a Scrum Master? (https://www.agilealliance.org/glossary/scrum-master/)

Burndown Charts (7.2)

The burndown chart at iteration level provides a day-by day measurement of the amount of work that remains in a given iteration or release. It tends to zero. By using the burndown chart the team can quickly calculate, the slope of the graph or the burndown velocity to estimate the expected delivery date.

The burndown chart at release level shows information such as: the work done in each iteration, the remaining work, the work done so far, and when it is expected to be done. Total effort is measured with the total story points.

Iteration Review (8)

At the end of the iteration there is an iteration review meeting.

During this meeting, the team shows what they accomplished during the iteration. The product owner, who is also in the meeting, reviews and gives feedback to the team.

Increment (9)

As a result of the Iteration review, there could be an increment in the features to develop, so there will be new user stories to be prioritized and be added in the product or release backlog.

Retrospective (10)

As each iteration comes to an end, it is important to have a retrospective meeting where the team can reflect on what went right and areas of improvement.

2. Main concepts for a traditional project

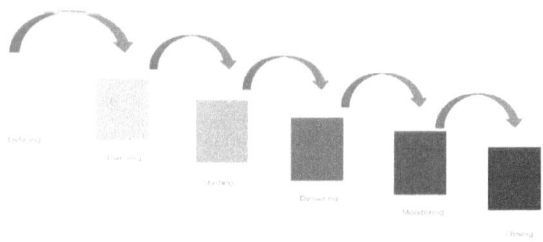

There are six stages to the traditional project.

Defining (1)

The defining phase refers to gaining a thorough understanding of the sponsor's business needs, and outline the solution, and how to deliver it. It also includes a definition of the context and the objectives of the project.

Planning (2)

During the planning phase the project manager develops the plan to a sufficient level of detail (at an activity level) to make reliable estimates and limit risks. This plan allows consolidating estimates, confirming the budget and overall schedule. It also allows obtaining the agreement from the project sponsor to launch project delivery start up.

Starting (3)

In the starting phase, the Project Manager expands the project plans to an operational level (task level) and begins the project execution.

Delivering (4)

In the delivering phase all the work is performed in a sequential way, ensuring all deliverables are delivered on time and in budget according to the approved plan.

Monitoring (5)

In the monitoring phase you, as Project Manager, perform any on-going work necessary to track and report on progress, as well as make periodic updates to key measures of project health. It is important that we identify the dependencies, risks, issues and control daily progress.

Closing (6)

Finally, during the closing phase, the PM performs the necessary tasks to properly close out a project phase or the project itself.

Chapter 4 - Seven practices when managing your project.

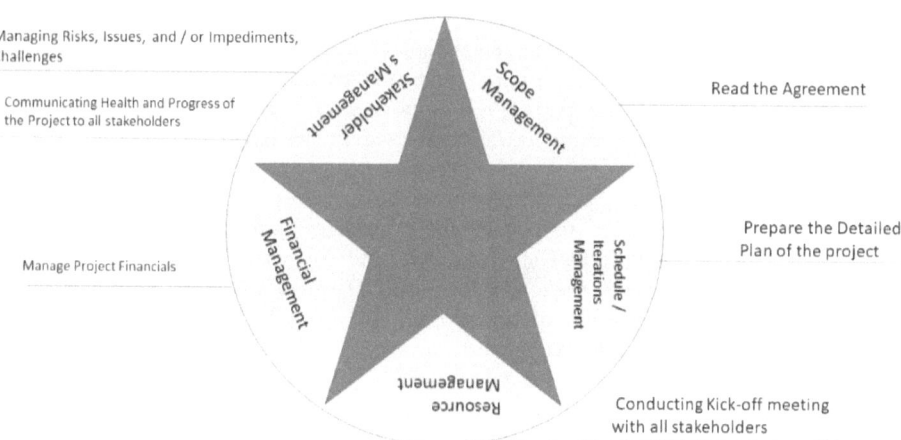

Managing Risks, Issues, and / or Impediments, Challenges

Communicating Health and Progress of the Project to all stakeholders

Manage Project Financials

Read the Agreement

Prepare the Detailed Plan of the project

Conducting Kick-off meeting with all stakeholders

Stakeholder s Management

Scope Management

Financial Management

Schedule / Iterations Management

Resource Management

1.	Read the agreement
2.	Prepare the detailed plan of the project.
3.	Conducting a Kick off meeting with all stakeholders
4.	Manage Project Financials
5.	Communicating Health and Progress of the project to all stakeholders.
6.	Managing risks, issues and/or impediments, Challenges
7.	Project Management Summary

Practice 1 – Read the Agreement

By reading the agreement, you get the understanding of the project – what has to be done, what problems are to be solved and by what commitments have to be own. The Agreement specifies the mutual commitments of the parties: the sponsor and the delivery organization, what approach will be used, and the contractual deliverables and milestones.

A typical agreement will have Statement of work(SoW)/ Scope, required Service Levels to achieve, applicable Charges need to pay by the customer, Third party Contracts (If any)/ Document of Understandings (DoUs), Hardware and Software requirements (if any) for executing the work, Site Details, Sections relating to Data Privacy & Security to take care while executing and after the completion of the project, Architecture of the solution, Exit Clause Contract change procedure, Service recipients.

Point to remember

Any document defines any of the commitments of the parties involved needs to be read and understood by everyone on the project.

Practice 2 – Prepare the detailed plan of the project

You are now ready to prepare the detailed plan of the project. You may have observed some high-level dates in the agreement   You have to identify tasks to meet the given dates in the agreement and set realistic timescales for the roles and effort involved.

In an agile project you will schedule iterations through user stories while in a traditional project, you will prepare a high-level project schedule with milestones and deliverables.

With these best practices, you ensure:

The Project team can commit to the project plan. Agreements with the sponsor and suppliers have acceptable levels of risk. Work can be managed and tracked effectively.

Practice 3 – Conducting a Kick-off meeting with all stakeholders

You meet with every member of the project team including the main project stakeholders, both internal and external, to provide them with information on the project. This will ensure that they are all aligned with the commitments of the agreement. To prepare for the kick-off meeting, you need to summarize the contents of the Agreement and then meet with all project team members, internal and external. The primary material to cover in the meeting includes the Agreement commitments – what, by when (Time) and how. With that information, in the meeting, the project team members should then discuss what each item means to them.

Practice 4 - Manage Project Financials

The purpose of financial management is to assess cost, and as required by many business areas, the profit and revenue variances from the plan. You need to know if your project is meeting financial targets the business requires, the variances (if any) and the reason.

Practice 5 - Communicate Health and progress of the project to all stakeholders

Throughout the project, communication with your stakeholders is the key. Periodically, you must inform internal and external stakeholders about the health and progress of the project. This reporting is generally done through a project status report.

Practice 6 - Managing risks, issues and/or impediments, Challenges

Challenges is another best practice required to deliver a successful project.

You identify, analyze and respond to risk and issues throughout the life of a traditional project.

You manage impediments and blockers on Agile projects for the same result – to reduce risk.

Practice 7 - Project Management Summary (PMSS)

It's also referred as Project Management System Summary (PMSS).

When you have these practices, you can draft the Project management summary for your project.

Project Agreement, Schedule or Iterations, Financials, Project Status, and Risks / Issues or impediments – all of these combines to provide a summary of the project for all your stakeholders which can be used throughout the project to track the project's progress.

Your project management summary is the collection of plans and procedures, which direct all project management activity on the project.

For all projects please note, you start with a blank Project Management Summary template and complete it while you manage the project and complete the project management best practices.

Chapter 5 - Change Management

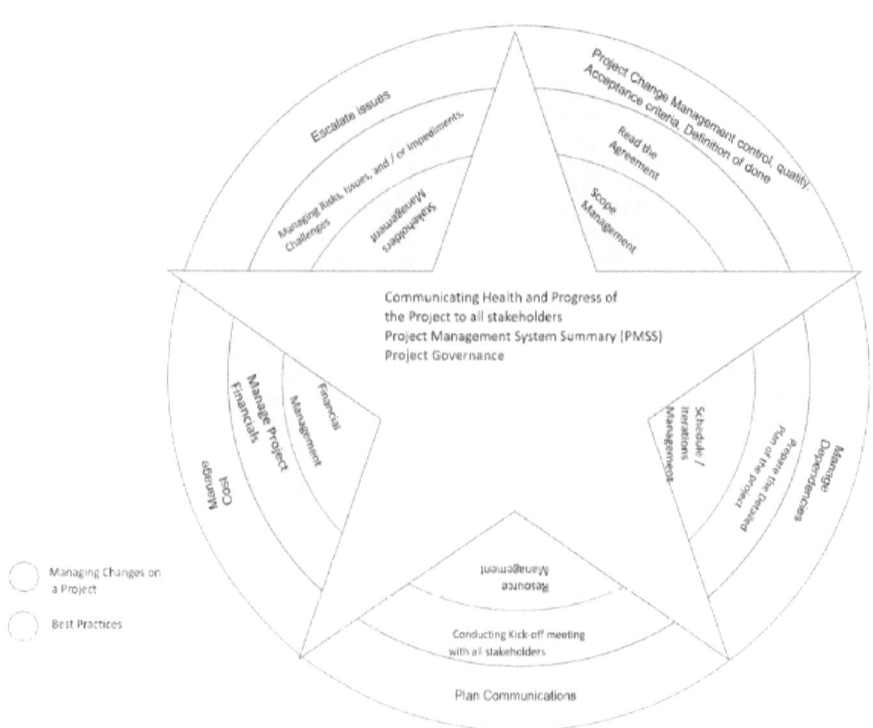

In this chapter we shall have discussions on

- Project change management
- Acceptance criteria and the Definition of Done (DoD)
- Analyze stakeholders
- Manage Dependencies
- Plan Communications
- Manage costs
- Escalate issues
- Project Governance
- Analyze stakeholders

1.   Project Change Management

Changes can and will happen at every point of the project lifecycle. Change include, but are not limited to, your client raising a request in a standup or status meeting, a stakeholder approaching a team member to make a change, a new government regulation may be enforced or align language used in the contract, etc. are some of the examples. All team members must be aware of the impact of change and be prepared to highlight changes when they occur so the changes can be handled appropriately.

Agile

Changes in requirements and priorities are part of the agile methodology. Just in time backlog refinement is the key to defining requirements, and hence there is no baseline established. However, there may be contractual baselines, for example, the number of iterations that comprise a release.

Points to remember

a. If you are starting a project, use the change management process outlined in the agreement or contract. Prepare the change management process for the project, if this does not exist, and get the customer confirmation to implement the same in the project.

b. Document roles and responsibilities for change and scope management, including a change management policy and escalation path.

c. Issue a Project Change Request immediately when there is a change.

d. No changes should be made until they have been approved. Document and track all changes from the original contract.

e. Get formal signoff of deliverables, formally communicate decisions and escalations, document meeting minutes, etc.

f. Do not accept informal agreements of changes.

2. Acceptance criteria

Acceptance criteria represent a specific and defined list of conditions that need to be met before a project's milestone can be considered completed and the project deliverables are accepted by the client. They can be criteria that include performance requirements and essential conditions, which must be met before project deliverables milestone are accepted.

These criteria should be measurable, achievable, and prove to our clients that our milestone is complete. Examples of some of the conditions or criteria of acceptance include

a. Completion of the Backup and Restore testing successfully
b. User acceptance testing (UAT) has been completed.
c. All requirements have been formally approved.
d. Acceptance criteria are usually defined at the start in the project scope document.

There are two main reasons why you should define the acceptance criteria and the definition of done in collaboration with your client.

a. You will be able to set the client's expectation level and lay the groundwork for their perception of the completed product.

b. Set specific billing condition of deliverables.

3. Definition of Done (DoD)

Definition of done is a checklist of the work that the team is expected to successfully complete before they can declare it to be shippable at the end of the iteration.

The Team owns the Definition of Done. It is a common agreement, built by the team and is shared between the Team and the Product Owner. Only the Teams are in a position to define it, because it asserts the quality of the work that they must perform.

Points to remember

a. Definition of done should be recorded and displayed prominently for the team to be able to visit before turning in their stories as complete.

b. Update the DoD when necessary during the iterations when the team has more understanding about additional items to include in the definition of done.

4.   Analyze stakeholders

Having committed, engaged, supportive and passionate stakeholders is critical to project success. Completing a stakeholder analysis helps you know where your supporters are, so you can define a strategy to communicate the right information by using the best channels for the audience.

Stakeholder analysis is the process of identifying the stakeholders involved in a project, determining their information needs and interests, assessing their influence, and formulating strategies to manage the relationships with them.

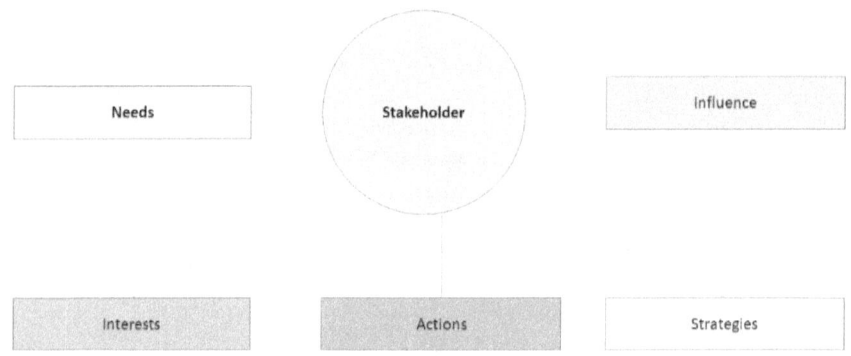

Points to remember

a. Identify all stakeholder and create an initial map. Rank the influence of the stakeholder.

b. Establish communications objectives for each of the stakeholders and document in the communications management plan.

c. Determine the information needs of the stakeholder constituencies involved in the project.

d. Manage and revise the stakeholder's analysis throughout the project life.

e. The stakeholder analysis is done at the start of the project. The stakeholder map is reviewed any time a stakeholder changes (new member, change of sponsorship, new roles responsibilities, etc.).

Impact of Stakeholders

5.   Manage dependencies

Dependency means when a task in the project depends on another task to start or complete and that dependency has an impact on the project in terms of resources, effort, schedule, cost, among others.

Dependencies can be of different types internal, external or both.

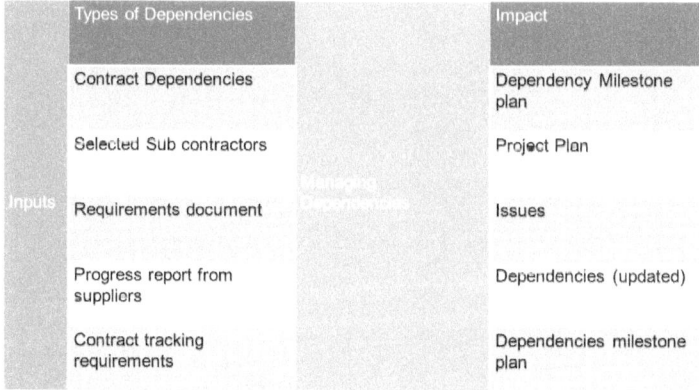

Types of Dependencies		Impact
Contract Dependencies		Dependency Milestone plan
Selected Sub contractors		Project Plan
Requirements document		Issues
Progress report from suppliers		Dependencies (updated)
Contract tracking requirements		Dependencies milestone plan

Points to remember

a. Identify dependencies by reviewing requirements and project plans including critical dependencies that can affect your ability to deliver.

b. For external dependencies negotiate the details of support required with identified supplier(s) and obtain agreement on the following items.

   o Detailed specifications for what to provide and in what format

   o The thresholds for managing critical dependencies and how to manage variances when the items are provided and in what sequence

   o The acceptance criteria of receiving group for work products delivered.

   o The process by which work products will be reviewed

   o Dependency reporting and tracking criteria (frequency and intensity)

   o Issue escalation process

   o Management of changes that affect commitments

c. Integrate all dependencies in the Project Plan

   o Integrate all dependencies in the project plan, reflecting dependent tasks and milestones.

   o The integrated project plan is then reviewed and approved by the project team and supplier

   o This approved integrated project plan is used for tracking the progress of the contract.

d. Manage dependencies

   o Compare activities against the plan

   o Track critical dependencies against the agreed thresholds

   o Evaluate the effects of early/late completion of activities for impacts on future activities and milestones

e. Identify and report activities and potential problems to all appropriate stakeholders

f.   Update the Project Plan/Iteration plan with current status

g.   Periodically review progress. Review commitments to determine if they are being met

h.   Potential problems become risks and are evaluated and managed following the Risk Management procedure.

i.   Actual problems become issues and are managed following the Issue Management procedure. Escalate when necessary.

6.   Plan communications

Communications are key to the success of any project, keeping the team connected and current on what's happening on the project and what's changing. Providing project communications helps ensure that all stakeholders have a solid understanding of the project and its implications.

- Communications planning includes identifying:

- Who needs what information?

- When they will need it?

- How will it be delivered?

Points to remember

a.   Start formal communications from day one.

b.   It is reviewed whenever change occurs in the stakeholders.

c.   Document minutes for every formal meeting.

d.   Define the right attendees for each different meeting

e.   Changes, Scope, Schedule, Cost Impact and Risk/Issue are mandatory, in Client communication meeting.

f.   A comprehensive communication plan influences the success of your project.

g.   Regular updates to all project stakeholders keep everyone current and aware of what is happening in the project.

h.   Defining how, what and when project information will be communicated - helps to mitigate communication issues which will hamper the success of the project.

i.   When clients bypass regular communication channels in order to expedite project tasks, team members should reiterate the correct communication channels and redirect the client accordingly.

7.   Project Governance

Governance is typically at 3 levels Strategic, Management and Operational.   This involves meetings, escalation and decision-making.

- Strategic - Decisions about business strategy and direction are made in the Strategic layer, as well as overall governance and relationship performance.

- Management - comprises the business direction and overall project performance.

- Operational level - focuses on day-to-day development, production support, and delivery excellence.

The three-tier relationship model ensures that measurements and plans are integrated to meet customer requirements.

a.   All meetings should be defined, agreed, and documented. The attendees, agenda, and frequency of these meetings should be documented as part of the Governance Model.

b.   All meetings should be reviewed frequently to ensure that the right people attend the meetings and to agree to the agenda with the client.

c.   During the operational level meeting, key escalations are made and move up the escalation ladder.

Effective governance includes knowing who makes decisions, and how, and who is responsible for executing against decisions.

Project management focuses on -

- Planning
- Cost, schedule, and activity control
- Productivity and reporting
- Resource and people management
- Risks, issues, and impediments
- Scope, change, and quality control
- Financial management and governance

Whereas governance focuses on –

- Decision-making
- Commitment
- Prioritization
- Alignment
- Monitoring
- Mentoring
- Visible leadership
- Escalation

To measure how well your governance mechanism is defined and works, periodic management and steering committee meetings, as well as regular status reports and communications are done.

Points to remember

a. Identify the Project governance reporting and meetings requirements

- Identify all reports needed in the governance activities. A purpose, frequency, recipients, and the meeting where the report is discussed or presented are outlined for each report.

- Identify all meetings for governance activities in the meeting plan. The plan identifies the meetings specified in the Contract and that support the management of the interfaces, inclusive of meeting charters. It also includes the meetings calendar.

b. Identify connected organization charts

c   Establishing organizational interfaces for management and operation of the contract.

d. Establish roles and responsibility matrix

    o   The matrix will describe the roles, functions and authorities needed to operate the Governance Plan.

e.   Create a baseline document for implementation

f.   This document includes all the information related to the governance processes and plans and it is the baseline for the implementation management.

g.   Implement & maintain governance processes and plan include

- o   Program issues
- o   Contract deliverables
- o   Contract change
- o   Formal correspondence
- o   Client satisfaction &
- o   Performance measurement

Governance leads to value creation and reduced "cost of coordination" for all parties involved e.g.

Governance	Value
Transparent	Increases the efficiency
Aligned to business	Helps with escalation in case problem arises
Decision framework	Efficient resolution of problems
Effectiveness	Better scope management

8. Estimate accurately

An estimate is an assessment of the likely quantitative (Numbers) result based on experience and historical data from previous projects, if any.

It is usually applied to effort, project costs and duration, and ideally includes some indication of accuracy.

There are four states for the estimate:

a. Indicative
b. Proposed
c. Committed
d. Closed

This contrasts with the forecast, which is based on experience and data from the current project.

Points to remember

A. Traditional Approach

Two techniques for estimating are commonly used in traditional projects.

Top Down Estimation

Quantification of the project scope into a project size of some units (e.g. Function Points, Logical Transactions, Use Cases, …)

a. Apply rates related to sizing units.

b. May involve adjustments for architecture, technology, external interfaces, team experience and other engagement environment factors

Bottom up Estimation

a. Examine the details and complexity of the solution and the deliverables.

b. Assess the effort for each deliverable and add up

c. May involve specific adjustments for team experience, client dynamics, varying degrees of quality assurance, team leadership, etc.

B.   AGILE Approach

Agile estimation facilitates alignment between the customer and the delivery team. It focuses on the actual need and incorporates changes by backlog prioritization, enabling delivery of the most valuable features in each release. Estimating in agile is done differently when estimating in a short, medium or long term.

a.   Short term – Iteration planning

Agile estimation in the short term is focused on the team level where user stories are commonly estimated in Story Points. A story point is an abstract measure of effort required to implement a user story. In simple terms, it is a number that tells the team about the difficulty level of the story. Difficulty could be related to complexities, capabilities, risks, and efforts involved. Some techniques used are Planning Poker cards, T-shirt sizing (Small, Medium, Large)

b.   Medium Term – Release planning

Medium term estimation is based on modelling delivery capability for multiple iterations and possibly for multiple teams.

Once the development team establishes its velocity (completed story points per iteration) over the span of a few iterations, then it is possible to support Product Owner decisions by using established velocity to do effective release planning. Normally, the burn up chart dhow for every iteration how many story points we finished. Based on number of story points we plan for a release; we can tell approximately in which iteration is going to be delivered.

c. Long term – Large initiative estimations

Large initiative and product estimations are more complex when new teams are involved and there is no historical information. It could use various methods such as Delphi approach, expert's opinion, historical references, using velocity of the teams with similar skills, project complexities and associated risks.

We do estimation

- When the proposal is built

- Any time when the project manager receives a client request for a new scope / Initiative

- Any time when a Change Request is raised, and a detailed approach is needed.

9. Manage costs

Project Cost Management includes the required processes to ensure that the project is completed within the approved budget, delivering the contractual scope. Poor Financial Management in a project leads to: Leakage or loss of money, Bad visibility, Impact on the Business Unit (Organization performance)

Points to remember

a. Forecast your project costs

Must guarantee that each accrual is due. All non-accounted costs must be in the forecast. Verify Check for rate applied, number of hours invested, Expenses charged against Work Items, Taxes charged correctly etc.

b. Collect and validate the financial data

Collect and validate expense data, such as travel expenses, Labour cost, suppliers' costs of purchases, Training, Hardware, Software etc.

Validate invoices against the progress data against quotations.

c. Calculate earned value indicators

Determine earned value indicators and variances:

Planned value (PV), **Actual Cost** (AC) and **Earned Value** (EV),

Calculate Cost Variance (CV) = EV – AC

Schedule Variance (SV) = EV - PV

d.   Reconcile Project data with business systems

Determine the financial discrepancies reviewing all validated costs and determining the cause of the discrepancies such as not reporting data, Incorrect data due to improper handling or not fully understanding the data requirements, Taxes charged incorrectly etc.

e.   Re-forecast the actuals

Re-forecast the actuals for the remaining periods and until the Project completion. Calculate and compare the Estimated at Completion (EAC) of the project among the previous Financial cycle versus the current Financial cycle, to identify potential problems in the project's profitability.

The Forecast must contain the adjustments of undue accrual. The project manager should act to minimize undue accrual by Weekly controlling the hours claimed, Approving all vendor Invoices, and all the expenses

Points to remember

Poor Financial Management in a project leads to: Leakage or loss of money, Bad visibility to Project Manager, Impact on the Business Unit (Organization performance)

10. Escalate issues

The potential risk and issue categories calling for escalation as given below

- Project Objectives not defined properly
- Critical dependencies
- Ambiguous roles and responsibilities / clarity required
- Financial overruns/underruns
- Scope disagreements
- Project resources
- Inter-team conflicts

- Incomplete prerequisites

- Responsibilities and dependencies
- Software issues
- Licenses issues

Escalation # Title :	Owner of the Escalation : Date Prepared : Date issue was raised : Date issue needs to close by :
Issue Summary	Affected Deliveries / Timelines
Actions taken to date	
Proposed resolution	Customer View
Impact of not resolving the issue	Cost involved
Impact on customer Satisfaction	

Some of these categories might require a higher level of intervention because the authority, decision making, effort required to resolve them on both sides.

Note

a. Escalation should occur when:

- The parties do not agree on a course of action
- A course of action is unsuccessful
- The parties have exhausted options
- Resolution is not achievable at project level
- Normally it is seen not more than 20% of the issues are escalated.

b. Documenting Log and document

- Notifying your superior on a (For your information) basis regarding critical issues before officially escalating them, gives them a chance to support the team in resolution of issues proactively and be aware of what is potentially coming.

- On the customer side, it gives the informed executive the chance to support personnel in achieving the desired outcome in a timely manner.

11. Relationships between counterparts (Service Provider and customer) of the ladder.

Manage the relationships between the counterparts of the ladder, between each stakeholder and their immediate superior in the ladder e.g.

Customer Organization involve in the Project	Relationship	Service Provider's Organization connected with the Project
Vice President Global	⟷	Vice President – Projects
⇕		
Vice President Project	⟷	Vice President - Project
⇕		
Chief Information Officer	⟷	Delivery Services Director
⇕		
General Manager – Project	⟷	Delivery Project Owner
⇕		
General Manager – Performance	⟶	Service lines Manager
⇕		
Solution Architect - Business	⟷	Technical SMEs

Project Management Best Practices for Project Success – Agile, Traditional & Hybrid

(Case Study)

Agile Project

Indian Software Alphabets (ISA) is a Bangalore, India based Systems Integration Company working for its customer XYZee, Hyderabad India, signed an agreement for the implementation of user authentication tool.

In this project ISA will deploy the tool User Authentication Manager (UAM), integrate with XYZee's existing cloud based Human Resources System and provide Hands and Feet support to XYZee.

The ISA team will be on-site for one week at the start of the project for the project initiation and one week at the end of the project for migrating the solution on cloud, & providing hands & feet support to XYZee's IT Team.

The project has been scheduled for 12 weeks and will start on a mutually agreed date June 1, 2020.

Scope

The services to be provided by ISA are

Sl. No.	Scope
01	Review and Confirm customer generated requirements
02	Build and Confirm environment setup and its readiness
03	Brief project team members on schedule, Scope, Deliverables and resources for the project.
04	Construct project Backlog
05	Plan Sprints
06	Specify and execute iterations (1-4)
07	Document Project Deliverables
08	Brief the client on Project Deliverables and do change-over to new solution
09	Provide the Hands and feet support for 2 weeks at customer's location

Roles & Responsibilities

Role	Number of Resources	Responsibility
ISA Project Manager	One	Project Delivery, Project Control and Tracking, Shareholders communication.
		He will also perform the Iteration Manager, Agile Team Leader and has the responsible for complete systems Integration
Agile SME	Two	Solution, Design, Development, Test and Delivery
Solution Architect	One	Support in Solution Design, Provide help during technical decision and technical issues resolution.
XYZee- Product Owner	One	Customer's Primary Interface with the team.

Deliverables

Sl. No.	Deliverable Name
01	SDD – Solution Design Document
02	PCD – Project Configuration Document
03	Test Cases and Test Results
04	Weekly Status Report
05	Cloud Migration Document
06	Product Backlog

Kick-off meetings

Two kick-off meetings have been held.

Sl. No	Kick-off Meeting	Key Agenda
01.	With the Team	To introduce the purpose of the project, Key roles and responsibilities, High level iterations plan and dependencies already identified, and the communication plan
02.	With the customer	Quick introduction to discuss logistics and all the key steps to follow to start the project.

Financial Plan

As per the business case, the revenue for this project is $ 70,000. A typical Gross Profit is 25 %. Approved expenses for travel and living are $ 8, 000

Sl. No	Line item	Value
01	Revenue of the Project	$ 70, 000
02	Travel and Living expenses	$ 8, 000
03	Gross Profit	25 %

Use specific best practices in an agile project

Manage Iterations

Planning a project is done differently in Agile and Traditional projects.

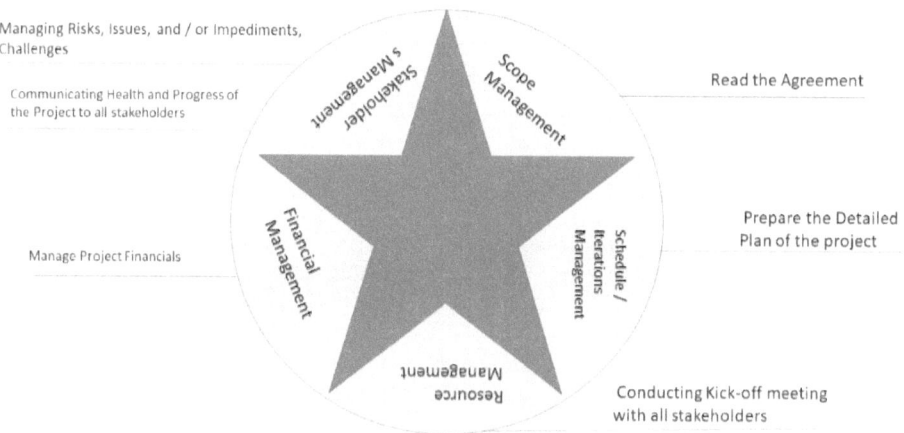

What is an Iteration?

An iteration, is a timebox in which development takes place. A typical time duration is 1 - 4 weeks, ideally 2 weeks. The duration is usually fixed for the length of the project. Each iteration produces an output that customer can potentially use.

What is Manage Iterations?

Managing iterations means managing the 'release roadmap', to visually communicate high-level planned milestones and dependencies.

How this has to be done?

An Agile approach focuses on the planning of each iteration. After an iteration is finished, the project team identifies the scope for the next iteration.

Work packages are developed through one or more iterations in which teams run tasks that   can be completed within the set time period.

Verification of progress towards release roadmap is easy on agile projects and is needed regularly. Integration and verification of activities happen daily and can be determined by using iteration boards or health reports, which list tasks as "done," "to do", "in progress", or "overdue".

The Integrated Project Plan Management (IPPM) and the Integrated Project Schedule Management (IPSM) are important project and program management tools that greatly help to plan and schedule work efforts in large and complex projects with dependencies.

Why we have to do?

Agile scheduling is the process of deciding how to commit resources to work that is deemed of highest priority based on perceived value. It is designed to adapt, plan, deliver and improve.

With iterative development, with small work product releases and frequent product delivery, clients can provide regular feedback so the team can react timely to changes.

When we have to do this or what is the Periodicity of this exercise?

Release progress can be updated regularly on an integrated master schedule.

Iterations also use several other tools to track progress, including daily stand-up meetings and integration reports.

At the end of each iteration, data is analyzed to determine if certain estimates of user stories were under- or overestimated and to reflect on underlying reasons, to improve estimates and to further accurate commitment of subsequent iterations.

Building the Project Management System document (PMS) or Project Management System Summary (PMSS) of your project

At the start of the project, you know very little about the project. With each passing day, you learn more information about the project which is the basis of the Project Management System. Documenting that information about the project is done in a Project Management System Summary (PMSS) is a living document for anyone on the project. That is updated whenever anything about the project changes.

The following sections that you need to document as a part of the PMSS

1. Project Agreement & Scope
2. Roles and Responsibilities
3. Project Schedule, Deliverables & Dependencies
4. Financial Plan
5. Communications
6. Risks and Issues

You can use this PMSS as a preliminary status report.

Section 1: Project Agreement & Scope

The agreement between ISA and XYZee, the client for this agile project has been signed. The very first thing that you do is to 'Read the agreement'.

Given below the key statements from the Project Agreement which are included in this project's PMSS scope section.

A.   Project Agreement

ISA will install and configure User Authentication Manager (UAM) a user access authentication tool at the client location, integrate with customer's existing cloud-based HR System and migrate UAM to cloud. The ISA team will be on-site for one week at the start of the project to initiate the engagement, and again for one week at the end of the project to hand -over project deliverable and transition the solution to production. The project is scheduled for 12 weeks and will start on a mutually agreed date.

B.   Project Scope

Sl. No.	Scope
01	Review and Confirm customer generated requirements
02	Build and Confirm environment setup and its readiness
03	Brief project team members on schedule, Scope, Deliverables and resources for the project.
04	Construct project Backlog
05	Plan Sprints

06	Specify and execute iterations (1-4)
07	Document Project Deliverables
08	Brief the client on Project Deliverables and do change-over to new solution
09	Provide the Hands and feet support for 2 weeks at customer's location

Section 2: Roles and Responsibilities

Role	Number of Resources	Responsibility
ISA Project Manager	One	Project Delivery, Project Control and Tracking, Shareholders communication. He will also perform the Iteration Manager, Agile Team Leader and has the responsible for complete systems Integration
Agile SME	Two	Solution, Design, Development, Test and Delivery
Solution Architect	One	Support in Solution Design, Provide help during technical decision and technical issues resolution.
XYZee- Product Owner	One	Customer's Primary Interface with the team.

Section 3: Project Schedule, Deliverables and Dependencies

Here are the tasks from the high-level project schedule including major milestones.

No.	Activities	Days	Duration
	UAM deployment and integration for XYZee	63 days	June 1 – Aug 24, 2020
1	Project kick-off	1 days	June 1, 2020
2	Iteration – 0	1 days	June 2, 2020
3	Discovery - Requirements Gathering	3 days	June 3- June 5, 2020

4	Development - Iteration Plan	52.5 days	June 8- Aug 24
	Select and commit user stories (Epics) for product backlog	3 days	June 8 - July 10
	Iteration – 1	12.5 days	June 11- July 29
	Iteration – 2	12.6 days	June 29 - July 13
	Iteration - 3	12.3 days	July 13 – July 30
	Iteration - 4	12.1 days	July 30 - Aug 17
5	Product Delivery	0.5 days	Aug 17
6	Hands & Feet Support	5 days	Aug 18- Aug 24
*Note : Weekly Status Report from Project start to end of the project		63 days	

There is a more detailed plan, the iteration plan that drives the team on a daily basis, For Example in Today's stand-up meeting Raj (Developer) informed Project Manager that he had finished the coding for the user story # 1 so Project Manager can assign him the next user story (user story # 3) from the iteration backlog.

Product Backlog	Iteration Backlog	In Progress (Current Iteration)	Ready for Testing
	User Story #4	User Story #2	User Story #1

This is **the list of deliverables** for this project:

- Project configuration document
- Solution Design document
- Test results
- Status reports
- Change-over document
- Product backlog

Projects typically have dependencies which are usually sequential timing between tasks in order of occurrence or completion required in one task before another task can start.

In this project, the main dependencies are:

Dependency	Owner	Critical date	Project impact (scope, cost, schedule, etc.)	Status
Client requirements	Client PM	Project day 2	Schedule	Closed
Environment readiness	Client PM	Project day 6	Schedule	Closed

During the status meeting the client Project Manager explains the need to add a new user authentication feature in which a role will permit application permission assignment without administrator intervention. The client understands this is the additional requirement not a part of the agreed product features so a project change request has been raised. The change impacts in the project by adding 4 more days to the development plan changing the schedule. As it is an added feature, the client is happy to pay an extra $3000 for the effort changing the financials. Because this is an added feature for in User Authentication Management (UAM) tool to provide, the change is in scope.

Section 4: Financial Plan

When preparing a financial plan, you must first determine your Budget. In this agile project, you have a given budget and a number of working hours allowed for your team.

Resource/Skill	Estimated No. of hours	Rate per hour	Total
Agile System expert – Developer	300	$ 50.00	$ 15,000
Agile System expert – Developer2	250	$ 44.00	$ 11,000
ISA Architect	20	$ 150.5	$ 3,010
Project Manager / Iteration Manager	320	$ 74.00	$ 23,680
		Total Services	$ 52,690
		Total T&L	$ 8.000
			$60,690

Once you know your budget, you will track the evolution of the Budget by controlling the labor from your team and you will analyze the iterations progress by reviewing your burndown chart and the project velocity.

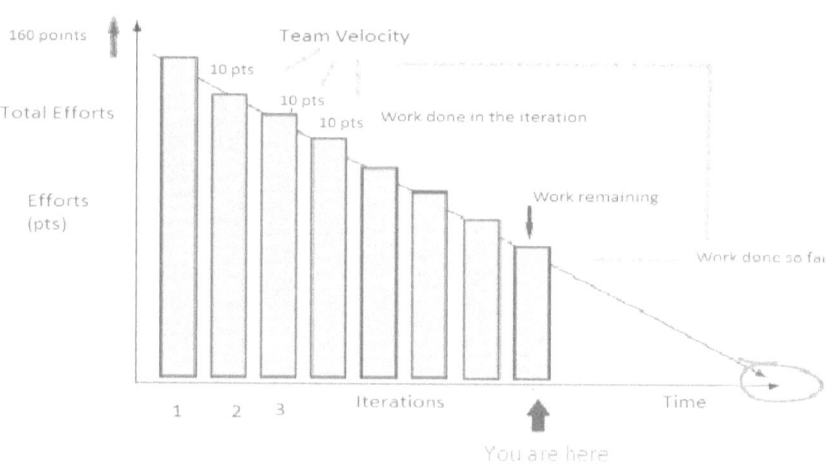

Section 5: Communications

Any project requires constant team communication. There are a lot of meetings that are held during the project execution.

In this agile project, the iteration duration is approximately 2 weeks.

Dependency	Owner	Critical date	Project impact (scope, cost, schedule, etc.)	Status
Client Requirements	Client Project Manager	Project day 2	Schedule	Closed
Environment Readiness	Client Project Manager	Project day 6	Schedule	Closed

Section 6: Risks and Issues

In the kick-off meeting with the client Project Manager, you learn that a key client technical resource is on an extended leave and is scheduled to return to work prior to the start of the engagement. If the return is delayed, the project start could be delayed.

Finding impediments during the project are quite common. During the testing of user story number 2, the Tester has identified that there is a type of role that is not working due to a problem in the Data Base. You decide to prioritize this impediment in your plan and assign it immediately.

Product Backlog	Iteration Backlog	In Progress (Current iteration)	Ready for Testing
	User Story #4	User Story #2	User Story #1

During the kick-off meeting, the customer informed that in the pre-engagement discussions with ISA Sales team, business requirements for the project were not completed. Client Project Manager is the owner for this issue.

Traditional Project

Traditional project scenario has been explained in the given 4 sections.

- Agreement
- Scope
- Roles
- Key deliverables.

Section 1: Agreement

ISA will provide Application Security on AWS Cloud (AppSoC) services for the deployment / migration of customer software (B-Analyzer) to be used for Business Analysis. The ISA solution scans the developer's code to determine if there are security vulnerabilities, rates them accordingly.

Up to 3 weeks after the deployment / migration, technical assistance will be provided to support the client during that period. The total duration of the project is 12 weeks.

Section 2: Scope

The services to be provided by ISA are

Sl. No.	Scope (Services)	Responsibility
1	Installation of the ISA product	ISA
2	Usage of the product	ISA
3	Reports generations of the result and interpret the results.	ISA
4	Customization,configuration and Administration of the product	ISA

Section 3: Roles

The team includes the following roles

Roles	Responsibilities
ISA Project manager	A Project Manager also acts as an ISA Engagement Manager. This person will coordinate, manage the engagement and control all performing activities.
ISA Senior Engineer	A Senior Engineer is responsible for products configuration and mentoring
Technical Security Leader	Gathering requirements. Documenting and creating the solution design document (SDD).
Post Deployment Assistant	Will provide technical assistance post deployment of the product.
Customer Project Manager	Single point of contact (SPOC) responsible for obtaining and providing information, data and take decision in a timely manner. He will also help in resolving issues at customer's end.

Section 4: Key Deliverables

Sl. No.	Deliverable
01	Solution Design Document (SDD) containing Deployment summary and information relating to Transfer
02	Regular status Reports

What do we know about the project?

a. Agreement

This project includes all the services required to deploy the Static Analysis capabilities at the client. It describes the technical assistance support deployment to the client for three weeks. It also states the duration of the project is 12 weeks, the key deliverables, responsibility from ISA and the client, a high-level schedule as well as the completion criteria and the total charges.

b. Project Kick-off

Two kick-off meetings have been held.

SI. No.	Kick-off Meetings	Purpose
01	With team	Introduce the purpose of the project, the roles and responsibilities, Project Schedule and Dependency
02	With customer	Quick Introduction and to share logistics and key steps to start the project.

c. Financial Plan

According to the business case, the revenue for this project is $100,000. A typical Gross Profit is between 25-30%, but in this case is 35% because ISA is using a sub- contractor a third-party support system. Approved expenses for travel and living is $8,000.

d. Use of specific best practices in a Traditional project.

i. Planning a project is done differently than the Agile project:
ii. Project schedule maps the project work along a timescale.

iii. With the Project Management schedule, you define the start date, end date and dependencies for all work units for which organization is responsible for.

These work units, together define the work to accomplish, are normally presented in a hierarchy of phases, activities, and tasks.

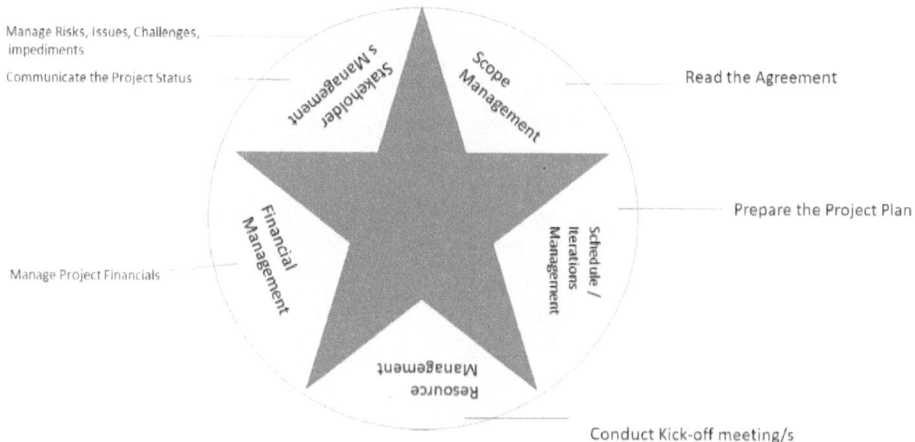

How do we do this?

i. Define project scope, which explains how the schedule is developed.

ii. Define activities to produce the project deliverables.

iii. Work Break Down (WBD) into activities - that provide a basis for estimating, scheduling, executing, monitoring, and controlling the project work.

iv. Identify milestones (significant points or events) for the project.

v. Sequence activities to identify and document relationships between the project activities and their dependencies.

There are three important inputs for your project schedule:

- Product Breakdown Structure (PBS)
- Organizational Breakdown Structure (OBS), and
- Work Breakdown Structure (WBS).

Why do we do this?

The Project Schedule provides an overview of activities for developing, monitoring, and controlling the project. It has phases for planning, developing, managing, executing, and controlling the project.

The schedule provides guidance and direction on how the project will be managed. You can monitor the status of activities and their progress.

The schedule also assists you to identify any deviation from the plan and to take actions to minimize the risk.

When or what is the periodicity of doing this?

Project Schedules are created at the beginning of the project and are then updated as and when change occurs. Any change that impact the schedule must have an associated approved change request.

e. Building the Project Management System Summary

At the start of the project, you know very little about the project. Each passing day, you learn more information about the project which is the basis of the Project Management System.

Documenting that information about the project is done in a Project Management System Summary (PMSS) – a living document for anyone on the project that is updated whenever anything about the project changes. There are following sections you need to document as part of PMSS.

- Project Agreement & Scope
- Roles and Responsibilities
- Project Schedule, Deliverables & Dependencies
- Financial Plan
- Communications
- Risks and Issues

A Scope of Work (SoW) has been signed as the agreement between ISA and the client. The very first thing that you do on a project is to 'Read the agreement'.

The key statements from the Project agreement which are included in this project's PMSS scope section.

Section 1: Project Agreement & Scope

ISA will provide Application Security on AWS Cloud (AppSoC) Services for the deployment of static Analysis capabilities into the client. Technical support up to 3 weeks also need to be provided to the client post deployment of the solution. The project duration is 12 weeks.

The solution scans developer's code to determine the existence of security vulnerabilities, and then categorize them accordingly (Severe, Low, Medium etc.).

The services provided are to assist with installing the product and enabling the client/developer/admin with to use the product, interpret the results, customize and configure, and administer the product.

ISA will undertake the following activities:

- Project coordination and Engagement management
- On-site AppSoC Kick-off and gathering requirements workshop
- AppSoC static Analyzer On-boarding and mentoring
- AppSoC post deployment and technical assistance.

Section 2: Roles and Responsibilities
Key roles and their responsibilities.

Roles	Responsibilities
Project Manager	Coordinates and manages the project, Using project management best practices.
Senior Engineer	Product configuration and mentoring.
Technical Security Leader	Follow-on post deployment deliverables.
Post deployment Assistant	Provide technical assistance post deployment of the product.
Client Project Manager	Interface between ISA Project Manager and the end users.

Section 3: Project Schedule, Deliverables & Dependencies

High Level project schedule is given in the table.

Sl. No.	Activities	Days	Duration
	Application Security of AWS Cloud (AppSoC) Services	39 days	
1	Project kick-off	1 day	June 1, 2020
2	Discovery - Requirements Gathering	2 days	June 2-3, 2020
3	Solution Design Document (SDD)	4 days	June 4-9, 2020
4	Product Deployment for testing in client's environment	20 days	June 10-July 7, 2020
	Creating the test environment for ISA	2 days	
	Deploy the product on test environment	1 days	
	Getting the access of customer system for testing	1 days	
	Testing, Share the results with customer post completion of the testing.	16 days	
5	Product Deployment in customer's Production Environment	10 days	July 8-July 21, 2020
6	User Orientation / Training	2 days	July 22-23, 2020

List of deliverables for this project are Solution Design document (SDD), Status and test results Report, and Product deployment.

The main dependencies are

Dependency	Owner	Critical date	Project impact (scope, cost, schedule)	Status
ISA access to customer's systems	Client Project Manager	June 11, 2020	Schedule	Open
Infrastructure (Server) setup complete	Client Project Manager	June 9, 2020	Schedule	Open

Customer wants to launch a new business application and would like to have it scanned also. A project change request needs to be raised in such situation.

This is a new business requirement that impacts the existing project schedule, project financials of the project. The schedule end date needs to be extended and we need to add 22 more hours of the developer's time for this new scan.

Section 4: Financial Plan

In the traditional projects, you have budget and working hours allowed for your team to put in the project. In a current situation

Roles	W1	W2	W3	W4	W5	W6	W7	W8	W9	W10	W11	W12
Senior Engineer			9	17	15	15	12	12	10	10	10	
Technical Security Leader	12	6		2								
Project Manager						12	10	12	10	8	8	5
Post Deployment Assistant									7	20	20	25

Resource/Skill	Estimated hours	Rate per hour	Total
Senior Engineer	110	$300,00	$33.000,00
Technical Security Leader	20	$310,00	$6.200,00
Post Deployment Assistant	72	$220,00	$15.840,00
Project Manager	65	$330,00	$21.450,00
		Total Services	$76.490,00
		Travel & Living	$8.000,00
			$84.490,00

Once you know your budget, you will track the evolution of the budget by controlling the labor from your team.

You can compare the hours planned Vs spent on the project to track / control the cost of resources.

Section 5: Communications

As a project Manager, you need to define all the communications in the PMSS indicating communication type, purpose, frequency, owner and participants

Communication Type	Purpose	Frequency	Owner	Expected Participants
Kick-off meeting	Overview of the project	At project start	Project Manager	One meeting with the internal team. Second meeting, with the team and the client
Project Status Review meeting	Review Status, Action Items	Weekly	ISA Project Manager/ Customer Project Manager	Entire Project team (Customer and ISAs)
On-site or remote workshops	Deliver tasks in SOW	As needed	ISA Consultant	Client technical consultant

Section 6: Risks and Issues

The following issues have been identified during the project:

Configuration needs to be changed to limit the report warnings for items that are par of the code and not detrimental to the security.

ISA consultant needs admin access of application in order to scan and provide fina report.

Summary

We have covered project management best practices which will help you to communicate more effectively on project scope, financials, risk, issues, impediments, challenges etc. As a project Manager of a project, the most important thing you can do is to communicate with all the stakeholders.

You can easily demonstrate project health, progress, and value of your project to your project stakeholders, executive sponsors, project team members and clients.

Glossary

A

Acceptance criteria

The definition of the results expected from the test cases used for acceptance testing. The product must meet these criteria before implementation can be approved.

Where a deliverable is subject to acceptance defined in an agreement, the set of conditions that the deliverable must meet for the deliverable to be accepted.

Agile project

Agile projects usually have fixed cost and schedule with variable scope.

Agile project plan

Set of committed user stories, the start and end dates for each iteration, and the project end date become part of the overall project plan and represent the agile portion of that plan. Plan relates to the schedule with committed stories.

Agreement

Used in a generic sense to cover any formalization of mutual commitments among parties.
The term agreement may cover:

- A legal contract between two distinct enterprises or organizations
- An internal agreement between two parts of the same enterprise or organization (e.g. a document of understanding(DOU)or a plan contract and offering proposal).

Note: The term agreement is also used to describe the initial agreement plus the sum of all amendments to date.

Audit

A systematic and independent examination to determine whether activities and related results comply with planned arrangements, and whether those arrangements are implemented effectively and are suitable to achieve objectives.

An audit focuses on analysis of evidence, followed by compulsory actions while an assessment is an appraisal with recommendations.

B

Budget

The total amount of labor hours and/or money allocated for a specific purpose during a specific period. Once approved, the budget is placed under change control and is the basis to establish the financial measurement baseline of
the project.

Build cycle

May consist of several iterations.

Results in a major checkpoint such as a configuration baseline, a milestone, a formal review with the customer, or an interim deployment to the stakeholders.

Ends with an integration test, review, and configuration management approval of the build as a basis for development in the subsequent build cycle.

Burndown chart

The burndown chart shows how quickly the agile team is completing the user stories. It shows the total effort against the amount of work the team delivers each iteration.

Burndown velocity

Velocity is the completion rate of the scrum team. It's usually measured in story points. In a burndown chart, it is represented by the slope of the graph.

Business case

A strategic document used to determine the effects a particular decision will have on profitability, by analyzing financial and cultural impact. A business case is typically used to justify levels of investment and guide decision making.

A business case should show how the decision will alter cash flows over a period of time, and how costs and revenue will change. Specific attention is paid to organization's rate of return (IRR), cash flow and payback period.

C

Change management plan

The change management plan defines the various types of changes (for example, small, in-scope, large) that may take place on the project and identifies what procedures should be followed for each type along with a clear definition of the criteria for each.

Contract

A legally binding form of commitment between parties.

Communications management plan

The communications management plan defines the regular meetings, reporting, and other communications that take place during the project. It identifies the type of information, the medium for communicating, and the audience to whom it is directed.

Compliance review

A review intended to ensure that standards, policies and procedures
are being followed by the project and to identify improvements to procedures.

Compliance reviews may be conducted by a dedicated organization within the company but external to the project, the sponsor, or an outside certification body such as ISO.

D

Daily stand-up meeting

In this meeting, the Team inspects their progress through the iteration so far and collaborates on the best way to proceed. It is not a status meeting in which the PM collects information about the progress, it is a meeting in which the team members commit to each other.

Definition of done (DoD)

Definition of done is a list of criteria that must be met before a user story/theme/release is considered as "done".

In order to be able to decide when an activity from the Iteration Backlog is completed, the
Definition of Done (DoD) is used. It is a comprehensive checklist of necessary activities that ensure that only truly done features are delivered, not only in terms of functionality but in terms of quality as well. The DoD may vary from one agile Team to another, but must be consistent within one team.

There might be different DoD at various levels:

- DoD for a Scrum Product Backlog item (e.g. writing code, tests and all necessary documentation)

- DoD for a sprint (e.g. install demo system for review)

- DoD for a release (e.g. writing release notes)

Deliverable

A work product that must be delivered according to an agreement.

Dependency

An input/output and/or time-related relationship. A project dependency exists between two project elements (for example, activity, sub-project, milestone). An external dependency exists between the project and an organization, activity, or event outside the project.

Deployment plan

The deployment plan describes the organization, strategy, resources, and methods used to deploy the new application at customer sites. The plan identifies the responsibilities of everyone participating in the deployment and is written from the user's perspective.

The deployment plan also serves as the project's master document over the migration period.

DoU

Document of understanding. The name commonly used for an agreement between two organizations belonging to the same company. (Internal to the Organization)

E

Effort

The number of labor units required to complete an activity or other project element. Usually expressed as staff hours, staff days, or staff weeks. Should not be confused with duration.

Estimation methodology

The quantified evaluation of the effort necessary to carry out a given development task.

F

Financial concepts

The following are key financial concepts you need to understand to manage your financials.

- **Revenue** - The money generated through product and service sales
- **Cost** - The value of money that has been used up to produce something, and hence is not available for use anymore.

Costs can be categorized in:

- Labor
- Vendor expenses
- Travel expenses
- Other costs

GP - The difference between revenue and the cost of providing a service, before deducting overhead, payroll, taxation, and interest payments.

$GP = Revenue - Costs$
$GP\% = GP / Revenue$

Financial plan

The financial plan is a set of one or more two dimensional tables that show the estimated and budgeted amounts for project expenditure and revenue by expenditure type and accounting period.

The plan may be presented at several levels of detail, depending both on the stage of the project at which it is produced, and on the intended audience, as well as, the level of detail required for the financial measurement baseline (FMB).

Financial management plan

The financial management plan is a documented plan on how revenue and expenditures will be tracked and controlled against the budget (financial management baseline) for a project, the approval process for expenditures and project forecasting.

Forecast

Predicted measurement of value, as opposed to actuals.

I

Impediment

An impediment is an obstacle that would cause a delay or waste to the project. Impediments or issues represent unplanned activities.

Impediment log

The impediment log is a list that identifies all impediments or issues that occur and require recording and tracking during the life of the project.

Iteration

A grouping of repeatable activities based on a set period of time that produces an expected set of results that has value. These results may be further refined in successive iterations.

Sets detailed increment goals for the development of specific functionality. The iteration includes design, implementation, unit test, and assessment.

Ends with an assessment of how well the increment goals of the iteration were met and approval of the software produced by the iteration for integration into the build.

Each build cycle may have multiple development teams working on parallel iterations.

The working software is of high quality and is shown to stakeholders. Outcome is to produce a set of functional deliverables that are accepted by the product owner and add value to their organization.

The feedback is used to improve the product in the next iteration. The amount of work done (velocity) is used in planning the next iteration.

Iteration manager

Refer Scrum master.

Iteration planning meeting

In this meeting, the team decides how much of the backlog it will commit to complete by the end of the iteration, based on the product owner's prioritization, and comes up with a plan and list of tasks on how to achieve it.

Iteration review meeting

The purpose of this meeting is to demonstrate what the team has built and generate feedback which can be incorporated into the backlog.

Issue

A term for a matter of concern on a project.

M

Master Agreement (MA)

A master agreement, or MA, is a contract reached between parties, in which the parties agree to most of the terms that will govern future transactions or future agreements.

Milestone

A significant event in the project or sub-project, such as a major decision, completion of a deliverable, or meeting of a major dependency (like completion of aphase).

P

Product backlog

Prioritized list of project requirements.

Product backlog meeting

The purpose of the meeting is determining the plan for the whole project. It is held at the start of the project.

Product breakdown structure (PBS)

A hierarchical decomposition of operational work products into components. Each descending level of this decomposition represents an increasingly granular view of the constituent parts of the components and interfaces of the product.

Product decision structure

The project decision structure documents the decision-making processes which involve the project manager and other stakeholders such as the sponsor.

Project dependency management plan

The project dependency management plan covers the dependencies between the project team and their stakeholders.

Project escalation path

The project escalation path documents the escalation path to be followed for all project related issues, by role, name and rules of escalation, in accordance with the reporting channels identified for the project.

Project health

Project health indicates the ability of a project to meet its stated objectives (from both a business and a customer perspective). It focuses on the emerging trends and unhealthy signs that may lead to problems in the future, if action is not taken to address them.

Project Management System Summary (PMSS)

The management system for a project. It includes processes, resources, roles and responsibilities. It is documented as a collection of plans, procedures, and records that define and support the way the management of the project will operate. It is also called Project Management Summary Document.

Project schedule

A schedule that organizes into work units, groups of activities performed by project organizational units and allows project status and dependencies to be tracked.

R

Release backlog

A release backlog is a subset of the product backlog that is planned to be delivered in the coming release, typically a two to six-month horizon. It would contain the same type of items as on a product backlog.

Release plan

A high-level project document that defines the timing and contents of each solution release, in terms of the features or functions to be developed or components of the supporting infrastructure to be completed.

Release planning meeting

The purpose of this meeting is planning the iterations and target end date for the release. It is held at the start of each release.

Requirement

1. A capability needed by the user to solve a problem [in order to] to achieve an objective
2. A capability that must be met or possessed by a system or system component to satisfy a contract, standard, specification, or other formally imposed documentation.
3. A formally documented description of those sponsor's needs that must be addressed by the
   project.

Retrospective meeting

The purpose of the retrospective meeting is to present what's working and what could work better.

Risk

A potential event or future situation that can potentially affect, prevent, or limit a project's success. Project risks may be threats or opportunities.

Risk log

The risk log is a list of known and open risks to the project. It is sorted in order of severity and associated with specific response actions.

Risk management plan

The collection of risk responses for identified project risks. The purpose of the risk management plan is to document all the plans associated with a risk or set of related risks.

S

Scrum master

The Scrum Master is a servant leader who ensures that the team adheres to Scrum values and practices, including issuing invitations to daily scrums, sprint reviews, and sprint planning.

The Scrum Master normally does the following:

- Removes impediments
- Supports close cooperation across all roles and functions
- Shields the team from external interferences
- Typically facilitates the daily scrums; at the very least, he/she ensures that they occur
- Ensures that the team is fully functional and productive; facilitates Scrum Events as requested or as needed
- Coaches the organization in Scrum adoption and working with other Scrum Masters to increase effectiveness of Scrum
- Helps the Scrum Team understand the importance of clear concise Product Backlog items

Sponsor

An individual or an organization who has the authority to perform, delegate, or ensure completion of the following project commitments:

- Formalization of an agreement with the delivery organization.

- Approval to proceed with the start of the project or of a phase.
- Acceptance of the deliverables from the project.
- Spending for the cost/price of the project as specified in the agreement.

The sponsor may be internal or external to the project

Sprint

A type of iteration within scrum.

Sprint backlog

Output of sprint planning meeting - task estimates and owners assigned to tasks.

Sprint planning meeting

Meeting at the start of each sprint resulting in the selection of user stories.

Stakeholder

Individuals or organization who are involved in, may be affected, or who can influence the project activities.

Stakeholder map

A stakeholder map is a diagrammatic representation of the stakeholders involved in a project and their interests. It is useful to establish the degree of influence that stakeholders are anticipated to have over the life of the project.

Scope / Statement of work (SOW)

A description of products and services to be supplied to the sponsor by the delivery organization, or to the delivery organization by a supplier when these organizations are separate business entities or companies.

Status reports

Scheduled report that documents accomplishments, records current state vs. plan, forecasts future state and progress, and describes significant risks and issues. Project status reports may be created for the line of business management, the sponsor, and/or the customer.

Story points

Unit-less, relative measures of size. Used as part of agile estimating and planning.

T

Traditional project management

Traditional project management includes a set of developed techniques used for planning, estimating, and controlling activities. The aim of those techniques is to reach the desired result on time, within budget, and in accordance with specifications.

Traditional project management is mainly used on projects where activities are completed in a sequence and there are rarely any changes.

Team charter

This artifact sets the ground rules for the operation of the project team, and joining the team implies its acceptance. It is presented to the team at the beginning of the project, sometimes in what is informally called the "kick-off meeting", or it could be presented at the time a person joins the team.

It contains information about shared performance objectives, expectations about team behavior, rules of engagement, key roles and responsibilities, and useful information.

U

User stories

A requirement written from the stakeholder's perspective describing what the product needs to do. User stories are generally written from a value standpoint (As a <role>, I want to <goal>

sothatIcan<businessvalue>)

Work breakdown structure (WBS)

A hierarchical structured list of all the project activities, in which the work of the project is broken down as necessary, level by level, into smaller and smaller work units, to ensure that the full scope of work to be performed is understood.

Work product

Used to define and describe the items needed as input or created as output of one or more tasks that are the responsibility of a single role.

www.ingramcontent.com/pod-product-compliance
Lightning Source LLC
Chambersburg PA
CBHW020614220526
45463CB00006B/2585